3

Long Vowel Sounds

Super Crazy Fun

BIG KID PHONICS

WARNING!

Lots of crazy words!

Author: Matthew Hitch

Co-author: Sunok Moon

Illustrator: Matthew Hitch

Cover Design: Brittany Hitch

Layout Design: Matthew Hitch

Text Design: Matthew Hitch

Image Manager: Matthew Hitch

~~Vain Meglomaniac: Matthew Hitch~~

Credits Editor: Matthew Hitch

Image Manager Manager: S. Moon

Image Manager Manager Control: Absolutely no one

Artistic Arguer: Sunok Moon

Dishwasher: Matthew Hitch
(occasionally Sunok Moon)

Title: Captain Matt's Super Crazy Fun

Big Kid Phonics 3 Student Book

ISBN 979-11-93590-27-0

First published 2023

Published by Hitch Publishing

info@supercrazyfun.net

This textbook came about as the result of 20 years of trying to make kids enjoy learning English. It is designed around the use of the rhotic R and other characteristics of English pronunciation common in North America. We believe it can be used in other parts of the world as most phonics books can, and we are keen to hear feedback from anyone who tries this.

We want to make clear that the word "crazy" used in the title is in relation to any of the common definitions illustrated below, and does not refer in any way to the meaning "insane."

strange/illogical   **wild**   **unexpected**   **fun**   **unwise**

About the Authors:

Matthew Hitch has taught English in Korea for the better part of 20 years and holds a master's degree in applied linguistics. He clearly does not have a pig nose, and by most accounts is not at all malodorous. He also cuts a dashing figure according to his wife.

Sunok Moon prefers to go by the name Michelle, and is in fact quite scary as reported in the bio on the back of this book. She has a degree in English literature and has taught English in Korea for approximately 3 weeks longer than Matthew, who is writing this and finds it weird to refer to himself in the third person.

Contents

Welcome parents and teachers!

Thank you for considering our book. Phonics books are notoriously boring, so this is the last bastion of publishing where even the tiniest bit of creativity can raise the bar (sorry phonics book publishers, but it's true). With that said, we humbly offer you our content. We have also intentionally challenged convention in a few ways. Much of what we have to say may be used or discarded though, and these books can be used just like any other mainstream phonics book. We hope you will choose to use whatever you please and dispose of the rest.

Please allow us to explain just where our method of teaching phonics may diverge from mainstream approaches, and please do forgive us for sharing information from what is undeniably the most mind-numbingly boring and seemingly useless field of study, linguistics. Most phonics books are not written by scholars in the field of linguistics. They are mostly written by early childhood educators, so perhaps that's the first divergence. We'll start with how we sound out consonants. In linguistic studies it is not uncommon for consonants to be distinguished by using a vowel (usually "ah") on both sides. This means a "V" sounds like "ahvah" and an "F" sounds like "ahfah" and so on. Most phonics books distinguish consonant sounds without such preceding vowel, but they do follow with a vowel in the form of the schwa. This is fine for most consonants, but the ones that are able to be maintained until breath is exhausted can be confusing with a schwa where they end a word. It's mostly ESL students who feel this confusion, but we think it doesn't hurt to teach those consonants without a schwa to native speakers as well, so where "V" sounds like "və" in most phonics books, in our book it is presented as "vvvvvvv" with no schwa. We apply this to all long consonant sounds in our audio files (L,M,N&R are also presented as long with a tiny schwa sound at the end though). If you have read this far, we take our hats off to you. Most would be fast asleep by now.

The next divergence is our use of Magic E. We chose Magic E for the fun potential. The Split Digraphs just can't seem to hold a crowd. Magic E is no longer used in most educational settings for many reasons, but mostly because as a rule it cannot be defined clearly. We do mention that split digraphs are better though, mainly to extend an olive branch to all the teachers we hope will buy our books.

And the final divergence we would like to mention is our choice of words. Our choice of words may seem a bit odd at times throughout the books, but we chose them for their potential for keeping kids engaged over their usefulness. We approach a phonics book as a tool to teach about sounds much more than vocabulary. Poop, vomit, spit, fart, snot, and burp are the most popular with our students. We tried to find a spot for booger, but alas...

Our word choice is also strange in that it includes words that have the long E vowel when teaching split digraphs. Most phonics books glance over the long E vowel. The argument we have heard for this is that it is difficult for the younger students, but we suspect that it's avoided more because it's difficult for authors to find suitable words. We decided to give it a try, and our experience is that the long E words we chose are not that difficult for our students to grasp. Given that English is their second language, we believe native English speaking kids will cope with them just fine. Also you may notice our sight words are not all actually sight words - oops! Anyway, we hope you enjoy our silly books.

Welcome students!

Our friend E has a cool trick!
He can make his friends
A, E, I, O, and U say their names!

We call him Magic E!

It looks like fun, so we made a
rule that he is allowed to do it
if he wants to!

This is Magic E rule!

Magic E is also like a ninja!

He is silent!

But he can't just do it anytime he pleases!

He must be to the right of his friend, and in this book at least, there must be a letter between.

In your school, teachers probably won't mention Magic E.
They'll more likely use "Split Digraphs" for this rule.
That's actually much better, but Magic E is more fun!

Let's get started...

Sounds

Vowels

	Name	Sound

Tracks 0-9

A   a 

E   e 

I   i 

O   o 

U   u 

i and u can be very short!

Long vowel sounds

Long vowels are easy! They're just the same as their names!

But sometimes U cuts its name short.

Then its long sound is just "OO!"

Practice with your teacher:

1. at = Ate   2. et = Ete   3. it = Ite

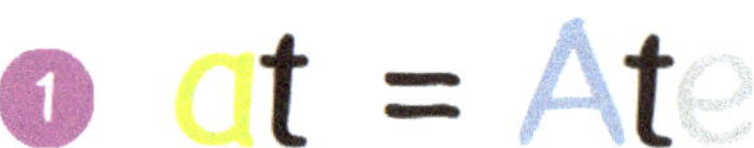 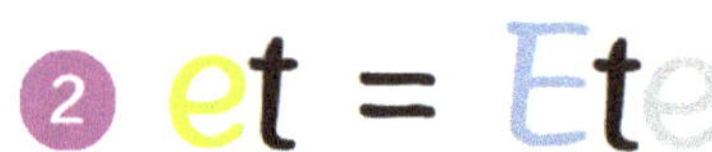

4. ot = Ote   5. ut = Ute

Consonants

"Sometimes Sounds"

Many letters have "sometimes sounds."

Sometimes C sounds like S.

Sometimes G sounds like J.

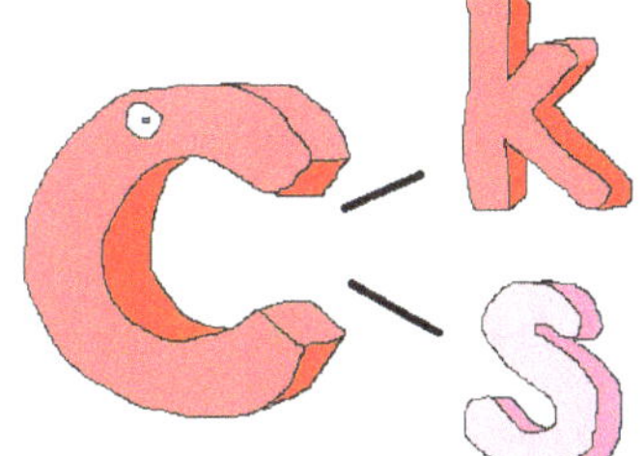

Magic E makes some consonants use their "sometimes sound!"

Sounds

Consonants

"Soft" sounds

Tracks 10-19

The softest alphabet sound of all is H, but don't think H is weak! H has the power to change others!

Track 12

When T is next to H it doesn't make its usual harsh sound. Instead, together they make this sound:

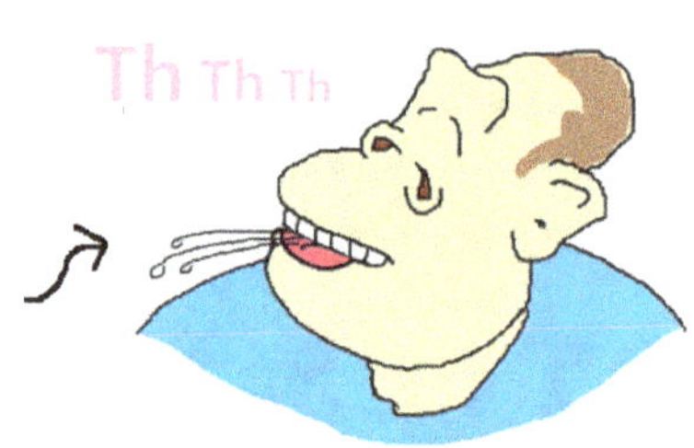

sh S and H together sound like this:

Track 13

ch C and H together sound like this:

ph P and H together sound like this:

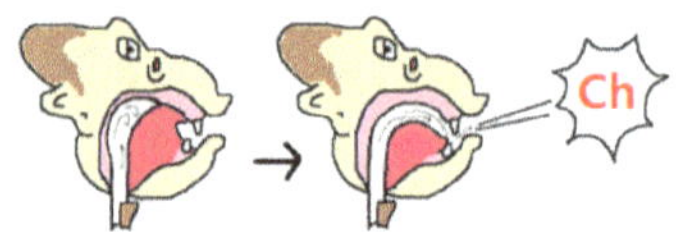
(same as **f**)

wh W and H used to sound softer, but not so much these days.

Consonants

Track
14

Tracks 10-19

Voiced and unvoiced sounds

Some letters have no voice. They are:

C F H K P S T & X

The rest of the letters use voice.

Sometimes voiced

Sometimes we say "th" with voice, sometimes not.

Track
15

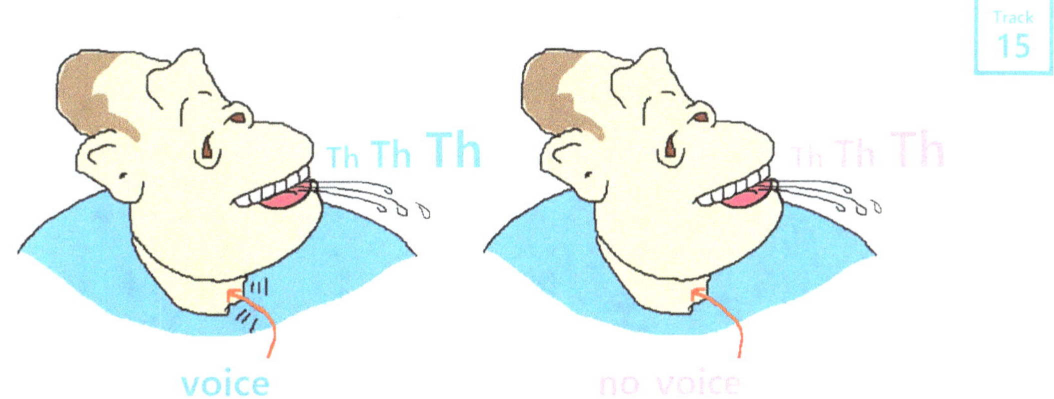

Sometimes S **just makes** Z**'s sound, even without any help from Magic** E**! That makes Z get really mad.**

Track
16

Listen, point, and make the sound:   Track 17 Words with  A

Tracks 10-19

1  ak  ake ake

2  am  ame ame

3  at  ate ate

Listen, point, and say: Track 18

1 cak + e = cake  cake

2 nam + e = name  name

3 hat + e = hate  hate

Follow the rules

Write the words

1   cak + e = __________ 

2   nam + e = __________ 

3   hat + e = __________ 

4   ap + e = __________ 

5   can + e = __________ 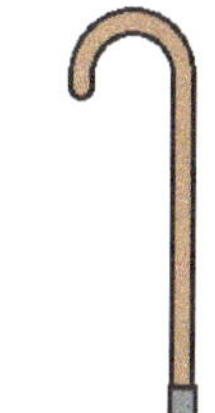

6   cav + e = __________ 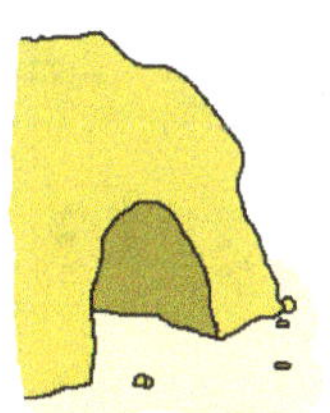

New Words

Listen, point and repeat the new words

ake

cake **lake** **rake**

ame

game **name** **same**

ane

cane **lane** **mane**

ape

ape **cape** **tape**

ate

gate **hate** **late**

ave

cave **save** **wave**

Exercises

Listen and write the last three letters

Track 20
Tracks 20-29

1  n _______

2  h _______

3 c _______

4 c _______

5 s _______

6 l _______

7 c _______

8 r _______

9 l _______

10 _______

Listen and circle the right letters AND picture

Track 21

1 ame ape ate  

2 ape ate ame 

3 ape ame ate  

4 ave ane ake 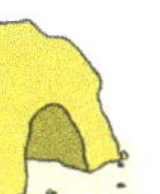 

5 ake ave ane  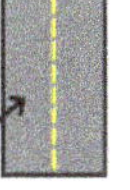

6 ane ake ave  

Exercises

Circle the word you hear

Track 22

Tracks 20-29

Circle the last three letters of the word you hear

Track 23

1. ame   ape   ate
2. ane   ake   ave
3. ame   ape   ate
4. ane   ake   ave
5. ame   ape   ate
6. ane   ake   ave

Chant

Track 24

That ape has the same name.
That ape has the same cane.
That ape has the same cape.
I hate that same name,
same cane, same cape ape!

Story

Write the word to match the picture

Listen and read along

Sight words: don't play take us first
brush bake with this we

Listen, point, and make the sound:   Track 26 Words with  E

Tracks 20-29

1  em eme eme

2 et ete ete

3 ev eve eve

Listen, point, and say: Track 27

1 mem + e = meme  meme

2 pet + e = pete  Pete

3 ev + e = eve  Eve

Follow the rules

Write the words

1   mem + e = __________ 

2   Pet + e = __________ 

3   Ev + e = __________ 

4   her + e = __________ 

5   gen + e = __________ 

6   them + e = __________ 

New Words

Tracks 20-29

eme

meme   theme

ene

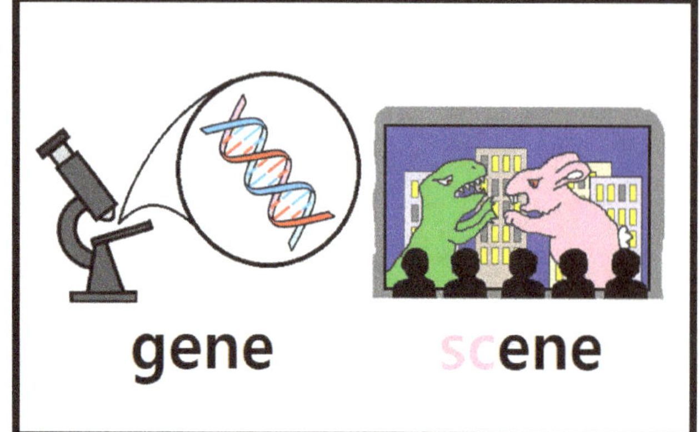

gene   scene

ere

here   mere

ese

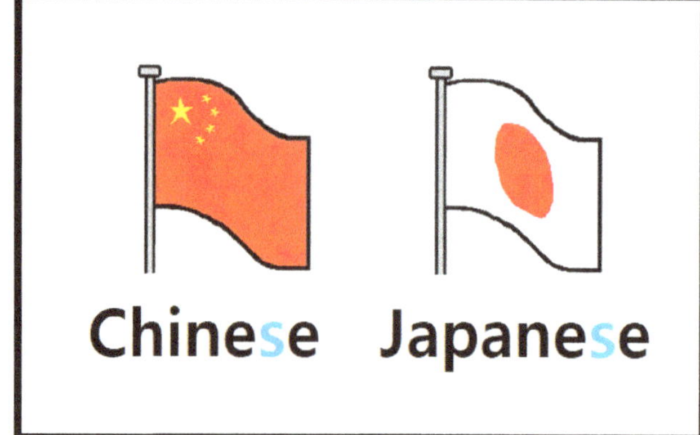

Chinese   Japanese

ete

delete   Pete

eve

Eve   Steve

Exercises

Listen and write the last three letters

1 h __________ 2 d __________

3 g __________ 4 m __________

5 St __________ 6 th __________

7 P __________ 8 __________

9 m __________ 10 sc __________

Listen and circle the right letters AND picture

1 eve eme ere  2 eve eme ere 

3 eve eme ese  4 ese ete ene 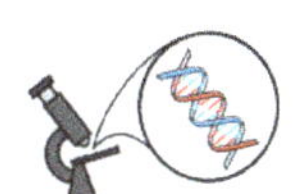

5 ene ere ete  6 ene ete ese 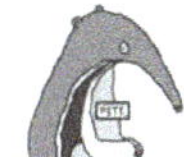

Exercises

Circle the word you hear

Tracks 30-39

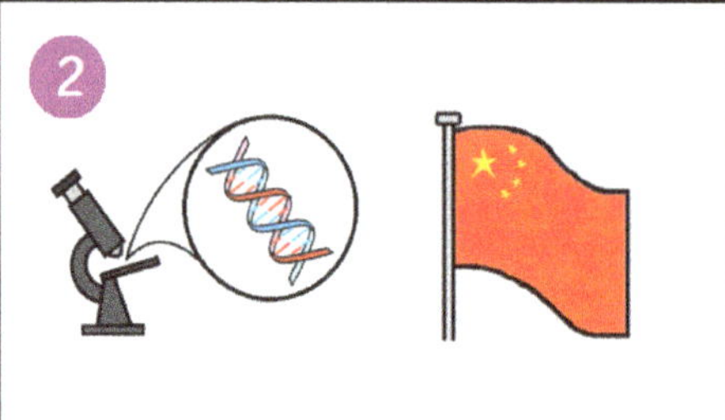

Circle the last three letters of the word you hear

Track 32

1 eve eme ere   2 ene ete ese

3 eve eme ere   4 ene ete ese

5 eve eme ere   6 ene ete ese

Chant

Track 33

Sight words: whose make

Eve's meme has a Chinese theme
Steve's meme has a Japanese theme
Whose meme will make the scene?
The meme theme scene is so extreme!

20   Unit 2

Story

Write the word to match the picture

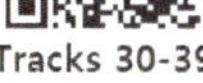

Listen and read along

Track 34

New words: new be best can leave supreme

UNIT 3   Long Vowel Sounds

Listen, point, and make the sound:  

Track 35   Words with  **I**

Tracks 30-39

1  ik    ike   ike

2 it   ite   ite

3  iv    ive   ive

Listen, point, and say:

Track 36

1  bik + e = bike    bike

2 kit + e = kite    kite

3 fiv + e = five    five

Follow the rules

Write the words

1 bik + e = __________ 

2 kit + e = __________ 

3 fiv + e = __________ 

4 rid + e = __________ 

5 lin + e = __________ 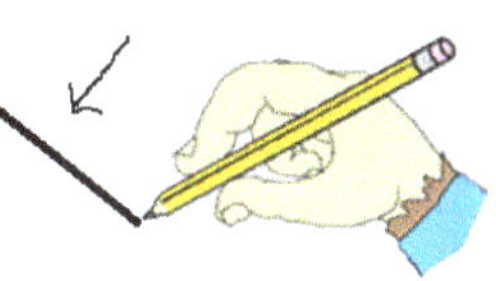

6 pip + e = __________ 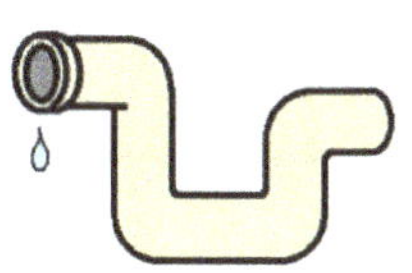

New Words

Listen, point and repeat the new words

Track 37

ide

hide   ride   wide

ike

bike   hike   like

ine

line   mine   nine

ipe

pipe   ripe   wipe

ite

bite   kite   site

ive

dive   five   hive

Exercises

Listen and write the last three letters

1 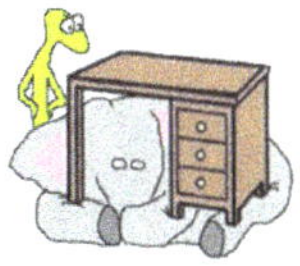 h ______

2 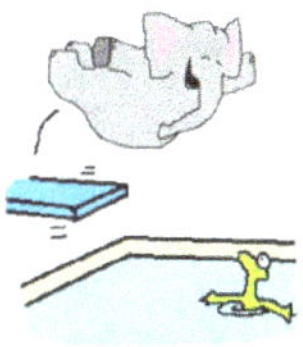 d ______

3 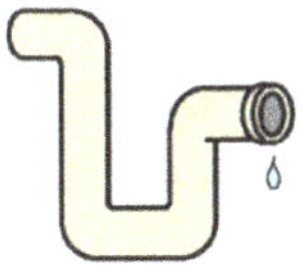 p ______

4 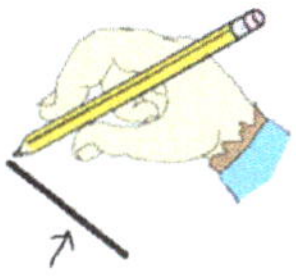 l ______

5 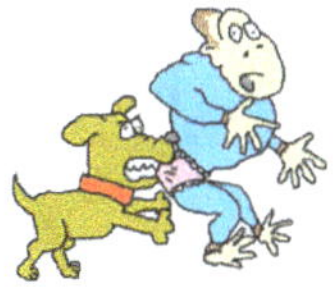 b ______

6 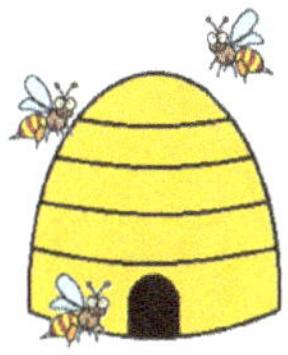 h ______

7 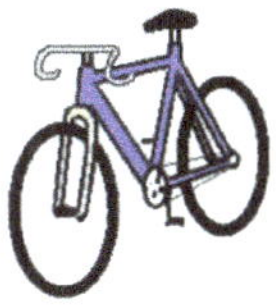 b ______

8 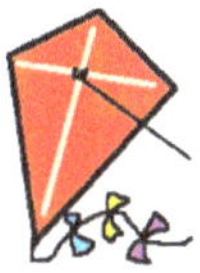 k ______

9 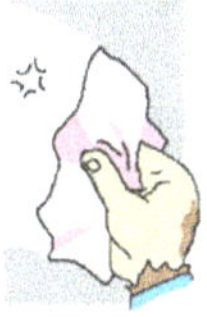 w ______

10 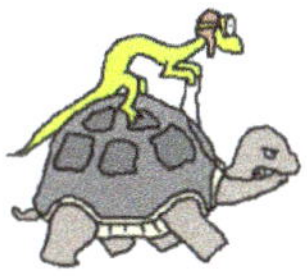 r ______

Listen and circle the right letters AND picture

1 ide   ike   ine 

2 ide   ike   ine 

3 ide   ike   ine 

4 ipe   ite   ive 

5 ipe   ite   ive 

6 ipe   ite   ive 

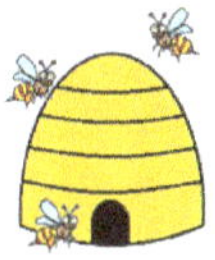

Exercises

Circle the word you hear

Tracks 40-49

Track 40

Circle the last three letters of the word you hear

Track 41

1. ide ike ine
2. ipe ite ive
3. ide ike ine
4. ipe ite ive
5. ide ike ine
6. ipe ite ive

Chant

Track 42

Sight words: at but after even

I like to hike and ride a bike.
Nine to five I'm at the hive,
But after five I like to hike.
I like to hike and ride a bike,
And maybe even fly a kite.

Story

Write the word to match the picture

Tracks 40-49

Listen and read along

Track 43

Sight words: next   hello

Review

1

1 cake   2 lake   3 rake

4 game   5 name   6 same

7 cane   8 lane   9 mane

2

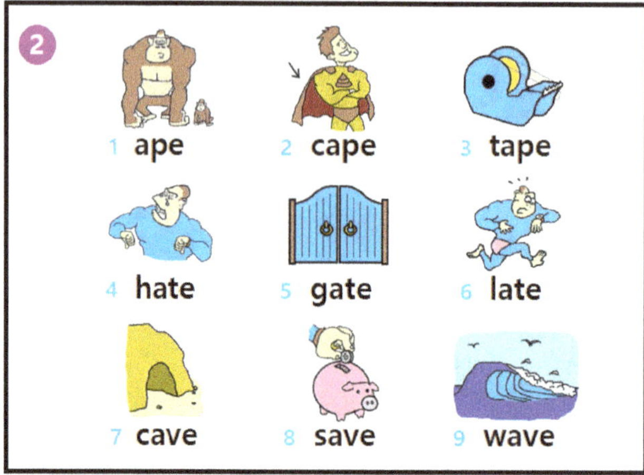

1 ape   2 cape   3 tape

4 hate   5 gate   6 late

7 cave   8 save   9 wave

3

1 meme   2 theme

3 gene   4 scene

5 here   6 mere

4

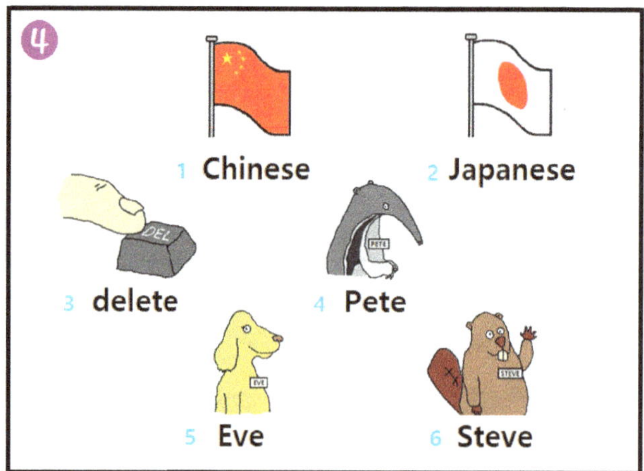

1 Chinese   2 Japanese

3 delete   4 Pete

5 Eve   6 Steve

5

1 hide   2 ride   3 wide

4 bike   5 hike   6 like

7 line   8 mine   9 nine

6

1 pipe   2 ripe   3 wipe

4 bite   5 kite   6 site

7 dive   8 five   9 hive

Review

Say the word and write it

1  _______________

2  _______________

3  _______________

4  _______________

5  _______________

6  _______________

7  _______________

8  _______________

9  _______________

10  _______________

11  _______________

12  _______________

13  _______________

14  _______________

15  _______________

16  _______________

17  _______________

18  _______________

Review

Find the path

A     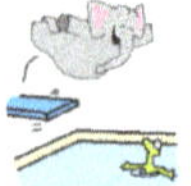    

E         

I         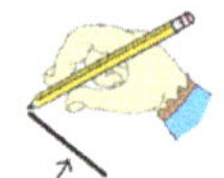

Listen to the final sound and circle the right picture

Track
45

Tracks 40-49

1	  			2	  		
3	  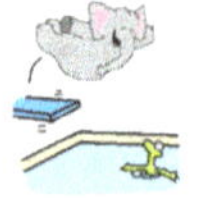			4	  		
5	 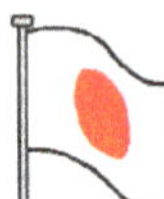 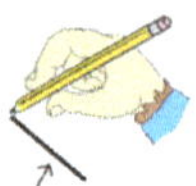			6	  		
7	  			8	  		

Review

Listen and circle. Then write the number in the word list.

Tracks 40-49

Pete		wide	
cane		gate	
ride		save	
ripe		here	
wave		kite	

When you finish the last one, shout "BANANA" very loudly and do a little dance.

UNIT 4   Long Vowel Sounds

Listen, point, and make the sound:  

Words with **O** 

Tracks 40-49

1  ol    ole   ole

2  on    one   one 

(Not to be confused with the number 1)

3  op    ope   ope

Listen, point, and say: 

1 mol + e = mole  mole

2 bon + e = bone 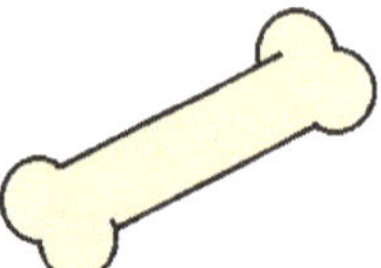 bone

3 rop + e = rope  rope

Write the words

1 mol + e = ________ 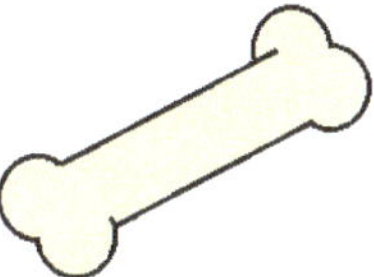

2 bon + e = ________ 

3 rop + e = ________ 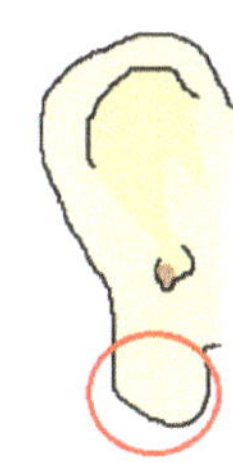

4 lob + e = ________

5 jok + e = ________ 

6 not + e = ________ 

New Words

Listen, point and repeat the new words

Track 49

obe

globe   **lobe**   **robe**

oke

joke   **poke**   **yoke**

ole

hole   **mole**   **pole**

one

bone   **cone**   **zone**

ope

hope   **mope**   **rope**

ote

note   **rote**   **vote**

Exercises

Listen and write the last three letters

1 h ______

2  r ______

3 h ______

4  gl ______

5 c ______

6 v ______

7 l ______

8 p ______

9 z ______

10 m ______

Listen and circle the right letters AND picture

1 obe oke ole 

2 oke obe ole 

3 obe oke ole 

4 one ope ote  

5 one ote ope 

6 one ope ote  

Exercises

Circle the word you hear

Track 52

Tracks 50-59

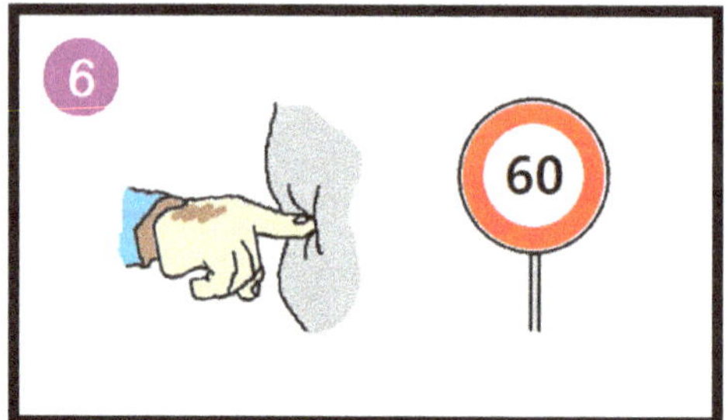

Circle the last three letters of the word you hear

Track 53

1. obe   oke   ole

2. one   ope   ote

3. obe   oke   ole

4. one   ope   ote

5. obe   oke   ole

6. one   ope   ote

Chant

Track 54

Sight words: for

Vote for mole! Vote for mole!
He's the best mole in the hole
All your hopes he will take note
Vote for mole! Vote for mole!
He's the best mole in the hole

36   **Unit 4**

Story

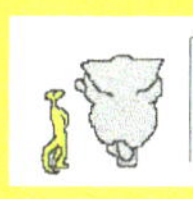

Write the word to match the picture

Tracks 50-59

____

____

Listen and read along

Track 55

Sight words: home room only also

UNIT 5   Long Vowel Sounds

Listen, point, and make the sound:  

Words with 

Tracks 50-59

1   ub    ube

2   un    une

3   ut    ute

Listen, point, and say:

1   cub + e = cub  cube

2   dun + e = dune  dune

3   cut + e = cute 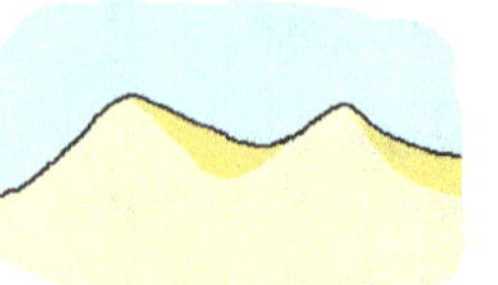 cute

Write the words

1. cub + e = _________ 

2. dun + e = _________ 

3. cut + e = _________ 

4. mul + e = _________ 

5. fus + e = _________ 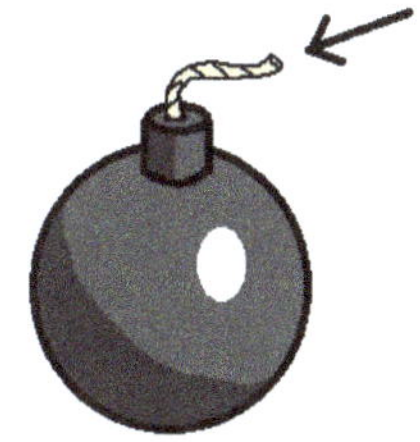

6. pur + e = _________ 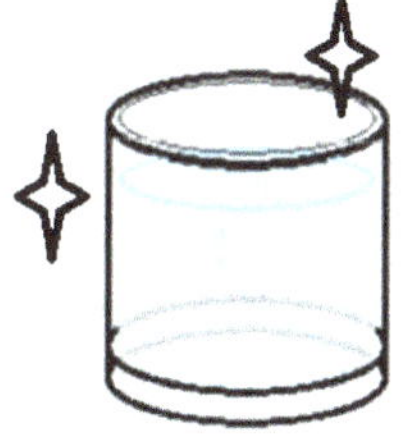

New Words

Tracks 50-59

ube

cube **jube** **tube**

ule

mule **rule** **Yule**

une

dune **June** **tune**

ure

cure **lure** **pure**

use

fuse **ruse** **use**

ute

cute **lute*** **mute**

Exercises

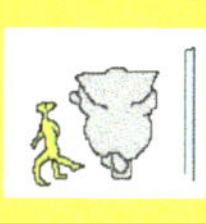

Listen and write the last three letters

1. t _______   2. d _______

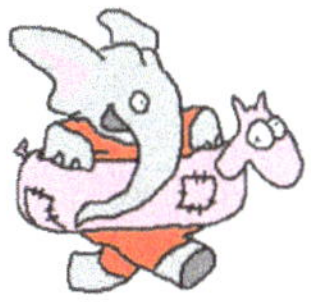

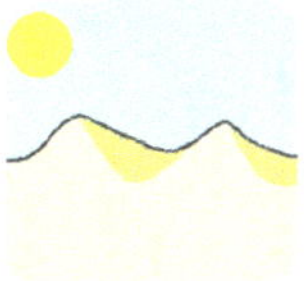

3. m _______   4. l _______

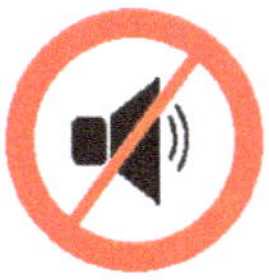

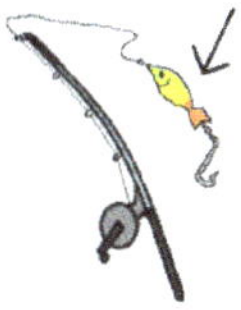

5. f _______   6. c _______

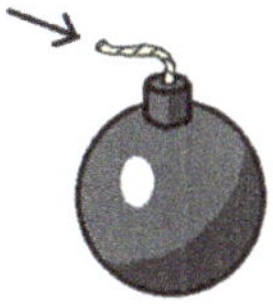

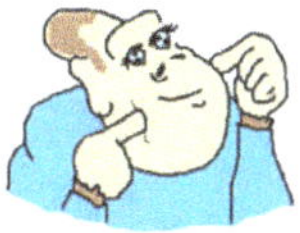

7. r _______   8. _______

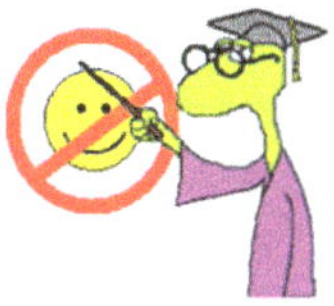

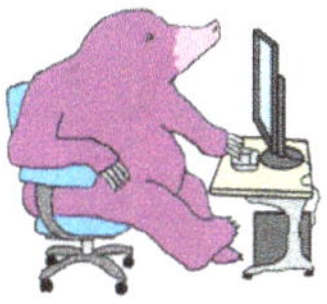

9. j _______   10. c _______

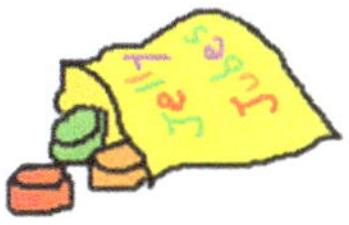

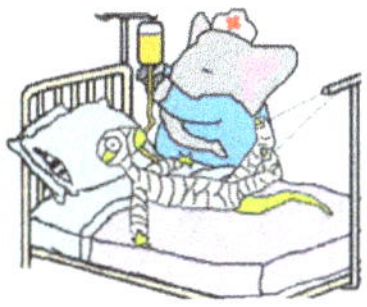

Listen and circle the right letters AND picture

1 ube ule une    2 ube une ule 

3 ube ule une    4 ure use ute 

5 use ure ute    6 ure use ute 

Exercises

Circle the word you hear

① 	② 	③ 
④ 	⑤ 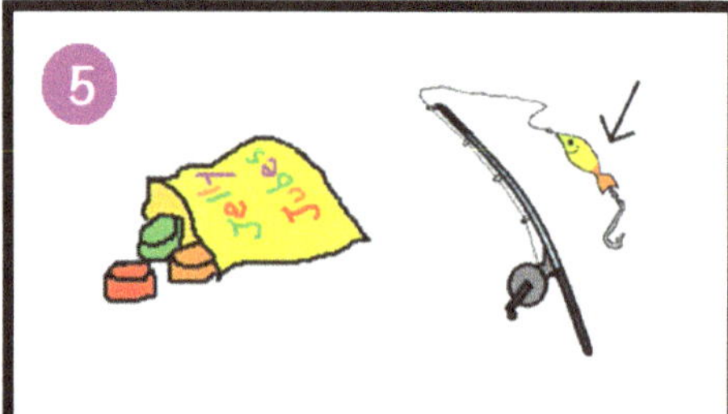	⑥ 

Circle the last three letters of the word you hear

① ube   ule   une   ② ure   use   ute

③ ube   ule   une   ④ ure   use   ute

⑤ ube   ule   une   ⑥ ure   use   ute

Chant

Sight words: can't

Cute mule plays a tune on its lute
Cute mule plays a tune on its lute
It's a ruse!
It's a ruse!
A mule can't play the lute!

42   Unit 5

Story

Write the word to match the picture

____

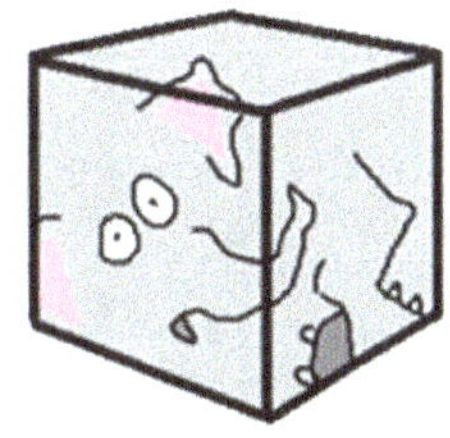
____

Listen and read along

Track 64

Sight words: is ate still soup

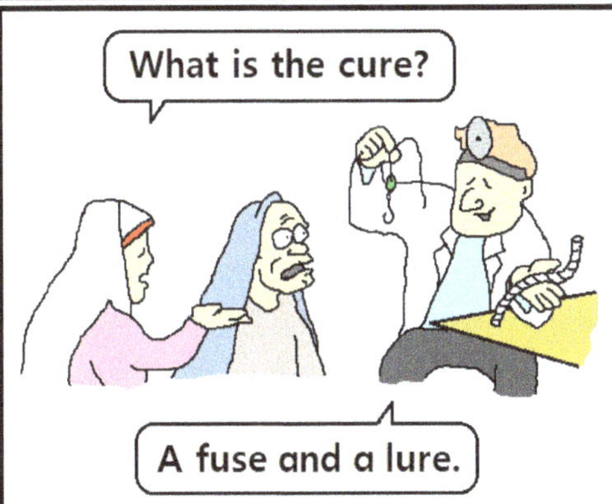

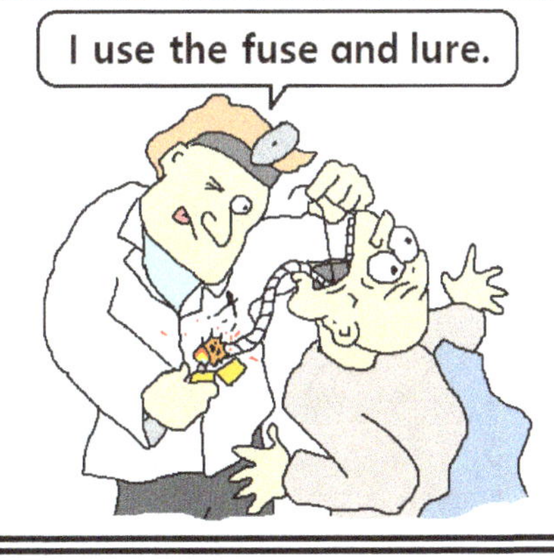

More Sounds

Tracks 60-69

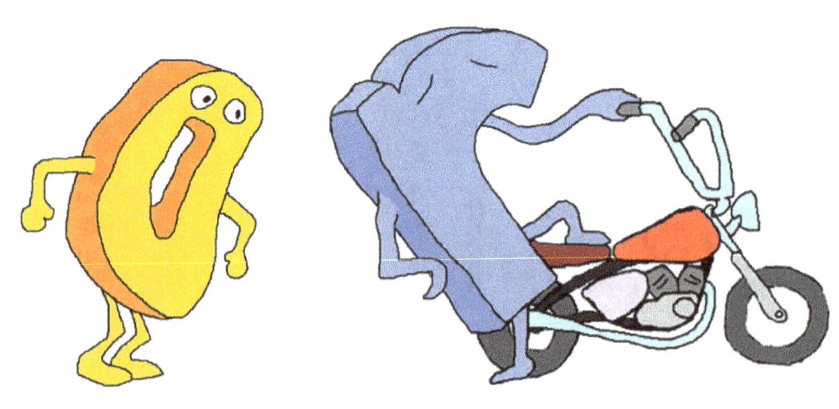

Sometimes E's magic just doesn't work. It never works on O when it's with R!

When they are together they completely ignore Magic E!

Practice with your teacher:

1 or, ore **2** for, fore **3** cor, core

Maverick words

Tracks 60-69

But it doesn't only happen with OR! A lot of words don't follow The Magic E rule.

Track
67

Spelling is crazy sometimes

Track
68

And some words seem completely free of ANY rules!

It's very strange.

UNIT 6   Long Vowel Sounds

Listen, point, and make the sound:  Words with A,E,I,O,U

Tracks 60-69

1   ad    ade

2   ac    ace

3   ir    ire

Listen, point, and say:

1   fad + e = fade 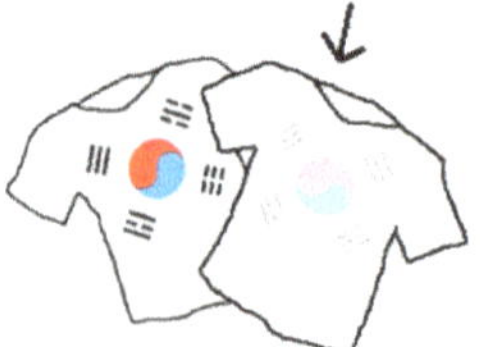 fade

2   fac + e = face  face

3   tir + e = tire  tire

Follow the rules

Write the words

1 fad + e = _______ 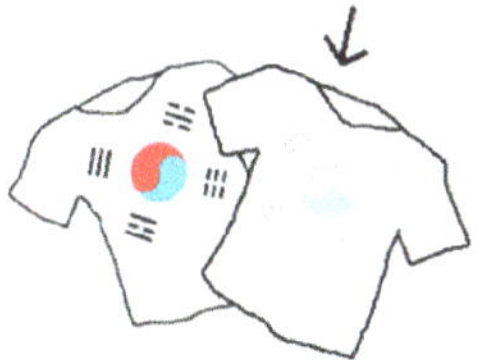

2 fac + e = _______ 

3 tir + e = _______ 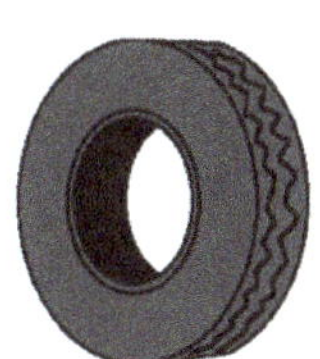

4 sor + e = _______ 

5 mad + e = _______ 

6 dek + e = _______ 

New Words

Tracks 70-79

Track 71

ade

fade made wade

eke

deke eke peke

ire

fire tire wire

ore

bore more sore

uke

duke Luke uke

c, g (magic E)

face huge nice

Exercises

Listen and write the last three letters

1 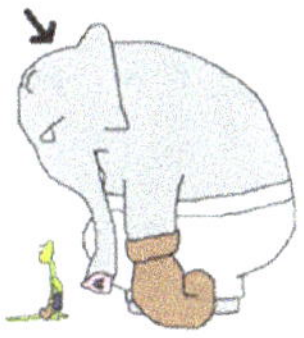   h __________

2 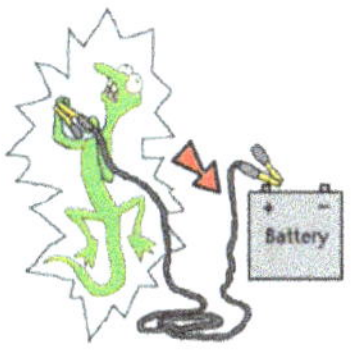   w __________

3 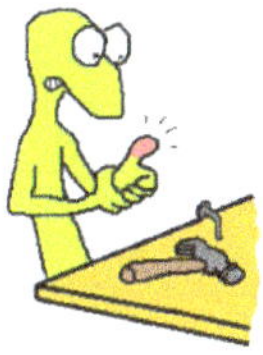   s __________

4 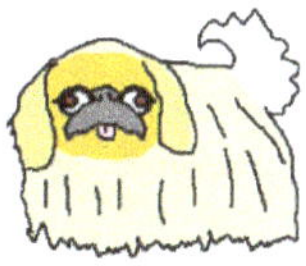   p __________

5 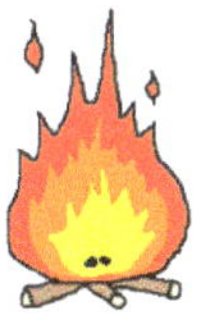   f __________

6 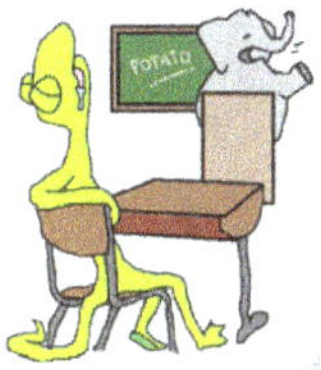   b __________

7   __________

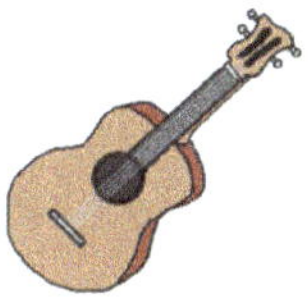

8 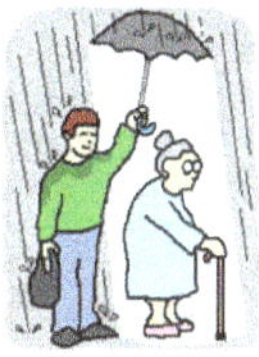   n __________

9 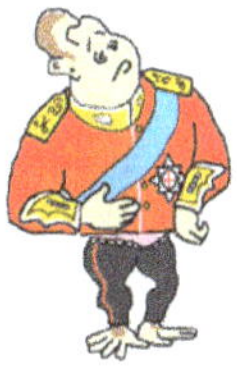   d __________

10 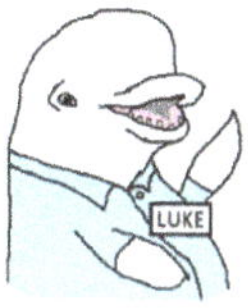   L __________

Listen and circle the right letters AND picture

1   uke   ire   eke 

2   ade   ice   ore 

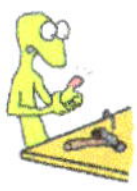

3   uke   eke   ade 

4   eke   ice   ire 

5   ire   ade   ore 

6   ore   uge   eke 

Exercises

Circle the word you hear

Track 74

Tracks 70-79

Circle the last three letters of the word you hear

Track 75

1 ade   ire   eke   2 ore   uge   ire

3 ace   ire   eke   4 uke   ire   ore

5 ade   eke   ire   6 ore   uke   ice

Chant

Track 76

Sight words: lit   people   yell   his

Duke Luke played his uke.
It made his fingers sore.
The uke wire lit on fire.
And the people yelled
"MORE, MORE!"

Story

Write the word to match the picture

Tracks 70-79

Listen and read along

Track 77

Words: poem into birthday walk maid never

The Story of Wh

Tracks 70-79

Long ago T, P, W, C, and S all softened their sound when they were with h.

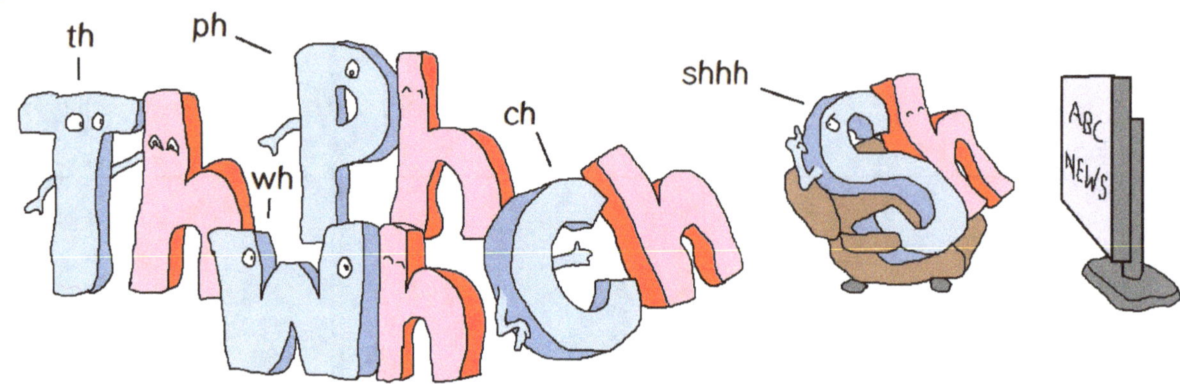

W was most polite! W even let h go first!

But as time passed W got very big

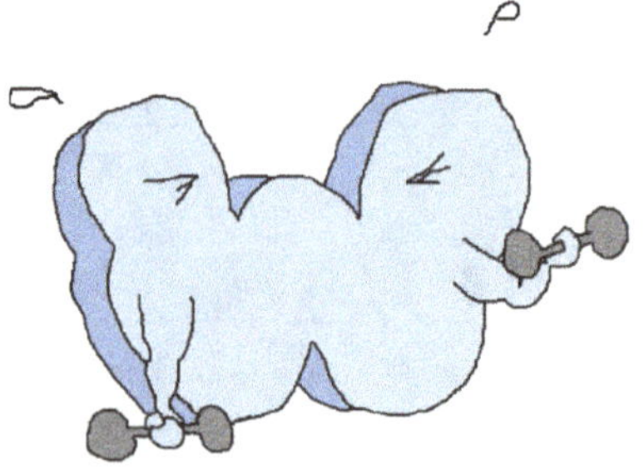

W soon forgot h was even there.

Strangely though, W is silent when they meet O.

Even More Sounds

"Wh" questions

Tracks 70-79

Long ago all the "wh" questions sounded the same:

What? → What?

When? → When?

Why? → Why?

Where? → Where?

Which? → Which?

Who? → Who?

(There is a 7th "wh" question, but HOW?)

Listen to the these words and repeat them

1. whale 
2. these 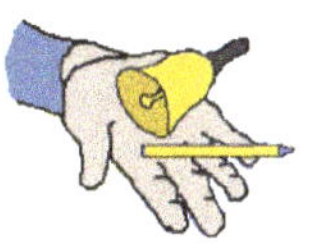
3. chide 
4. phone 
5. shute 
(Dubious form of "chute")

Isn't it cool you can read these so easily?

Review

Listen, point, and repeat all the words

Track 81

A

1 cake 2 lake 3 rake 4 game 5 name 6 same 7 cane 8 lane 9 mane 10 ape 11 cape

12 tape 13 hate 14 gate 15 late 16 cave 17 save 18 wave 19 fade 20 made 21 wade 22 face

E

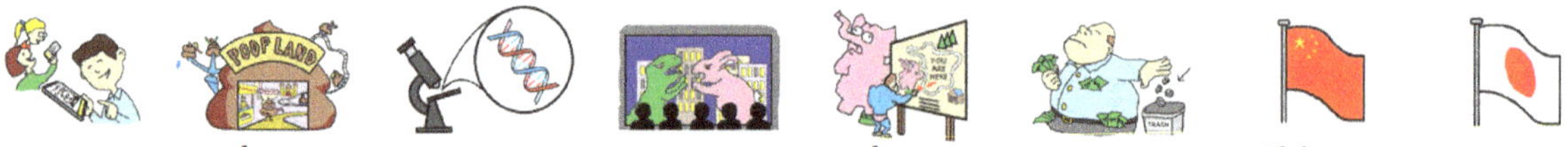

1 meme 2 theme 3 gene 4 scene 5 here 6 mere 7 Chinese 8 Japanese

9 delete 10 Pete 11 Eve 12 Steve 13 deke 14 eke 15 peke

I

1 hide 2 ride 3 wide 4 bike 5 hike 6 like 7 line 8 mine 9 nine 10 pipe 11 ripe

12 wipe 13 bite 14 kite 15 site 16 dive 17 five 18 hive 19 fire 20 tire 21 wire 22 nice

O

1 globe 2 lobe 3 robe 4 joke 5 poke 6 yoke 7 hole 8 mole 9 pole 10 bone 11 cone

12 zone 13 hope 14 mope 15 rope 16 note 17 rote 18 vote 19 bore 20 more 21 sore

U

1 cube 2 jube 3 tube 4 mule 5 rule 6 Yule 7 dune 8 June 9 tune 10 cure 11 lure

12 pure 13 fuse 14 ruse 15 use 16 cute 17 lute 18 mute 19 duke 20 Luke 21 uke 22 huge

Review

Say the word and write it

1. _______________
2. **9** _______________
3. _______________
4. _______________
5. _______________
6. _______________
7. _______________
8. _______________
9. _______________
10. _______________
11. _______________
12. _______________
13. _______________
14. _______________
15. _______________
16. _______________
17. _______________
18. _______________

Find the path

A       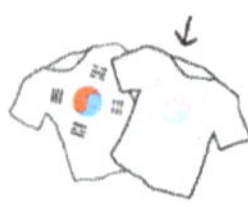  

E         

I     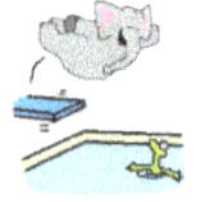    

O        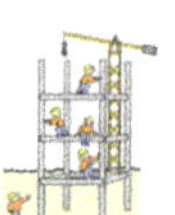 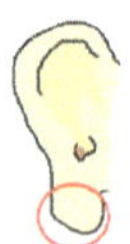

U 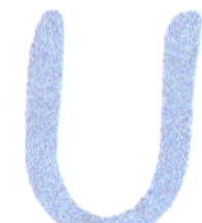        

Review

Listen and circle. Then write the number in the word list.

Track 82

Tracks 80-89

1 2 3

4 5 6

7 8 9

10 11 12

13 14 15

duke ☐	nice ☐	wipe ☐
poke ☐	tube ☐	late ☐
cure ☐	sore ☐	meme ☐
vote ☐	here ☐	fire ☐
made ☐	eke ☐	bike ☐

When you finish the last one, say "I'm so cute" until the teacher gets angry.

Test

Listen and circle the word you hear a Track 83 b Track 84 c Track 85

1        

2       

3 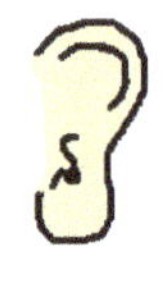      

4       

5    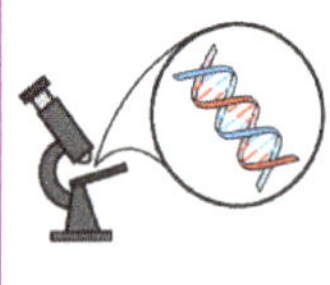 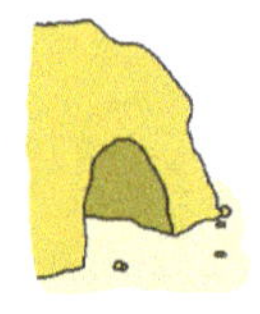  

6   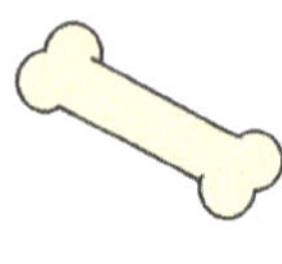    

7       

Test

Listen and write the long sound

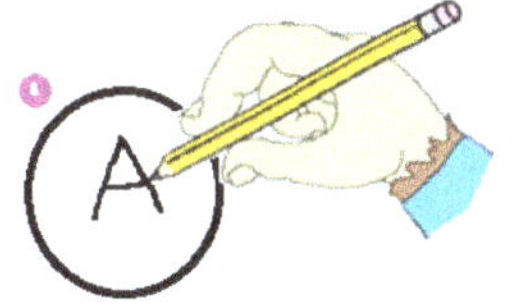

Tracks 80-89

1

2

3

4

5

6

7

8

9

10

11

12

13

14

15

16

Test

Listen and circle the last three letters a  Track 89 b  Track 90 c  Track 91

1  uke | ame | ole | ace | ere | ide

2  ate | ade | one | eke | ire | use

3  ote | ene | uge | ipe | ube | ake

4  ave | ine | eve | ute | oke | ite

5  ore | ape | ese | ope | ike | ule

6 eme | ure | ive | ane | ice | obe

Test  

Choose a picture and write the word to match

1 ________________________

2 ________________________

3 ________________________

4 ________________________

5 ________________________

6 ________________________

7 ________________________

8 ________________________

9 ________________________

10 ________________________

11 ________________________

12 ________________________

13 ________________________

14 ________________________

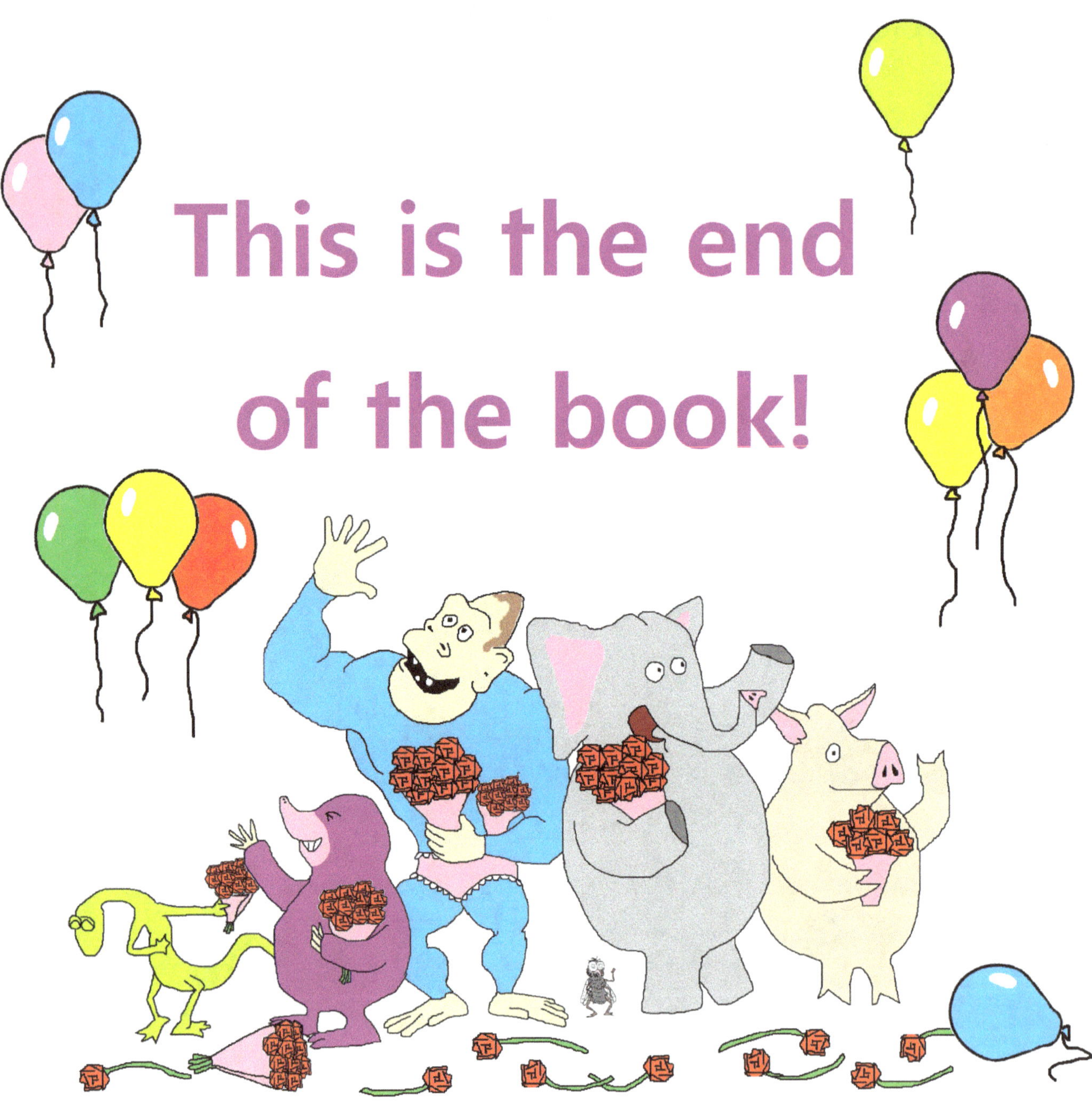

This is the end
of the book!

Word List

Unit 1

 cake    lake   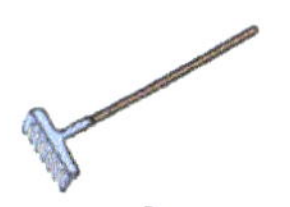 rake    game    name    same

 cane   lane    mane   ape    cape   tape

 hate    gate    late    cave    save    wave

Unit 2

 meme    theme   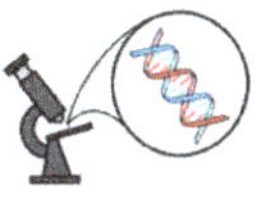 gene    scene    here    mere

 Chinese   Japanese    delete   Pete   Eve   Steve

Unit 3

 hide   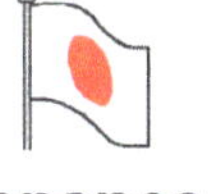 ride    wide    bike    hike   like

 line    mine    nine    pipe    ripe    wipe

 bite   kite    site    dive   five    hive

Word List

Unit 4

	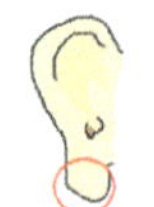			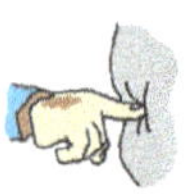	
globe	lobe	robe	joke	poke	yoke

hole	mole	pole	bone	cone	zone

hope	mope	rope	note	rote	vote

Unit 5

					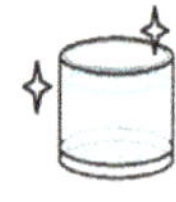
cube	jube	tube	mule	rule	yule

dune	June	tune	cure	lure	pure

fuse	ruse	use	cute	lute	mute

Unit 6

fade	made	wade	deke	eke	peke

fire	tire	wire	bore	more	sore

duke	Luke	uke	face	huge	nice

Our Sight Words

Word	Note (ESL)	Word	Note (ESL)
a/an		by	
and		fellow	
all		say	
on		go	
in		to	
the		win	
no		I	
lift		had	
like		it	
get		wait	
oh		have	
not		that	
did		yummy	
you		what	
your		she	
yes		wear	
my		so	
has		scary	
put		will	
one		fell	

Our Sight Words

Word	Note (ESL)	Word	Note (ESL)
down		many	
am/are		with	
want		call	
give		must	
me		now	
him		need	
shut		maybe	
he		P15 don't	
handsome		play	
pretty		take	
let's		us	
okay		first	
talk		brush	
do		bake	
or		with	
cent		this	
stop		we	
see		P20 whose	
too		make	
them		new	

Our Sight Words

Word	Note (ESL)	Word	Note (ESL)
be		lit	
best		people	
can		yell	
leave		his	
P26 at		poem	
but		into	
after		birthday	
even		walk	
next		maid	
hello		never	
P36 for			
home			
room			
only			
also			
P42 can't			
is			
ate			
still			
soup			

Phonics Series

Preschool:

Kindergarten:

Elementary School Junior:

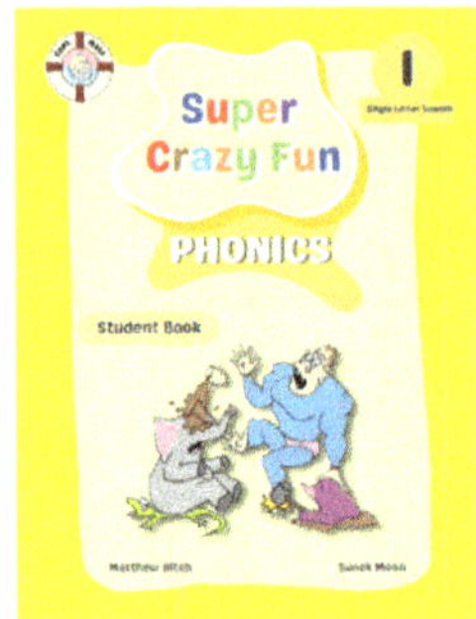 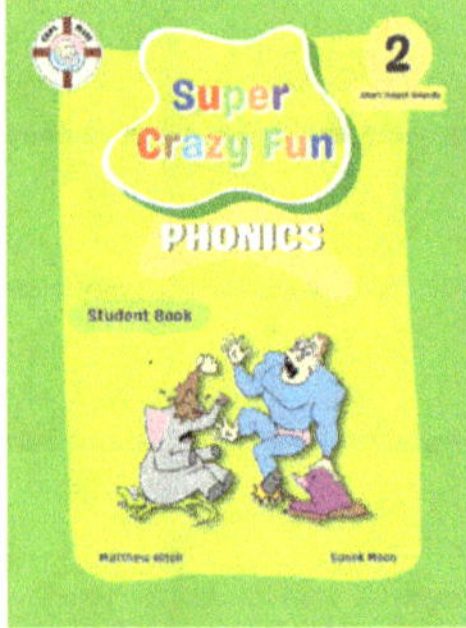 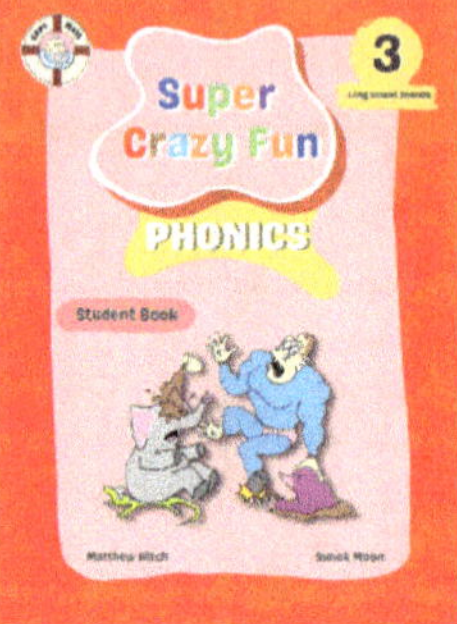 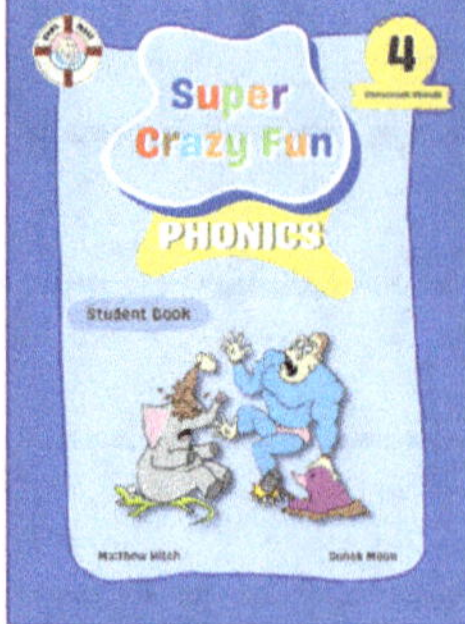 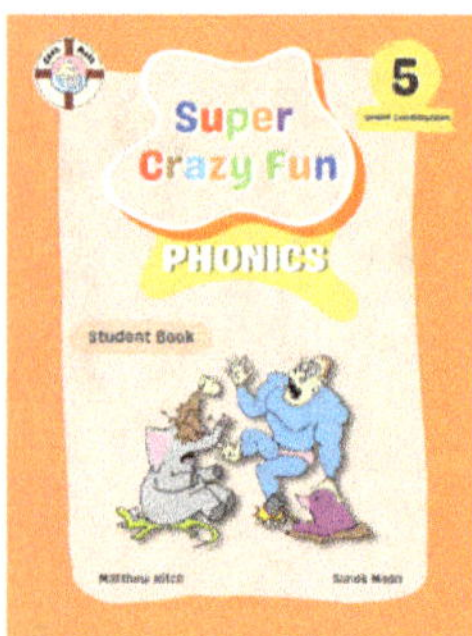

Elementary School Senior/Remedial:

  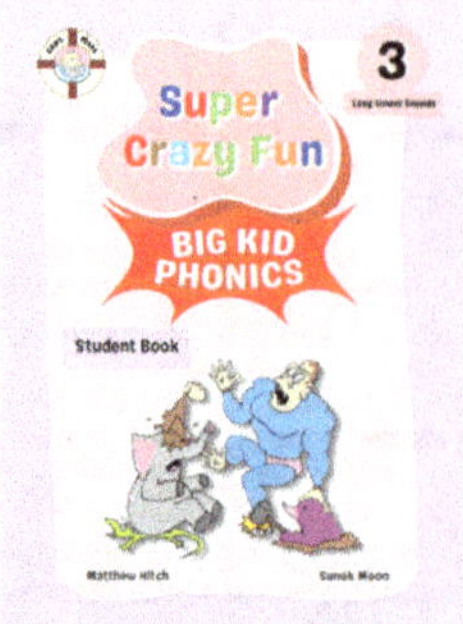 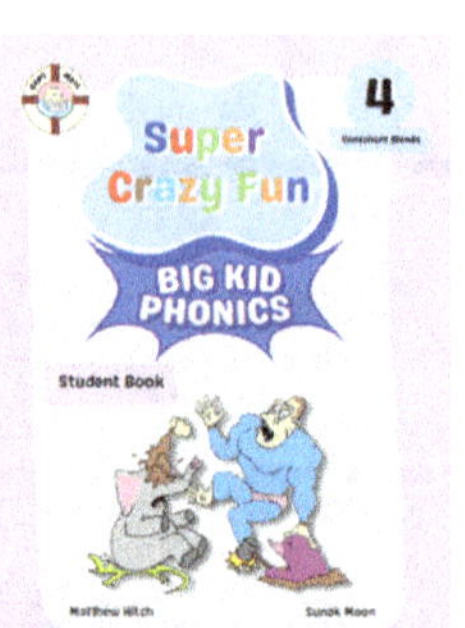 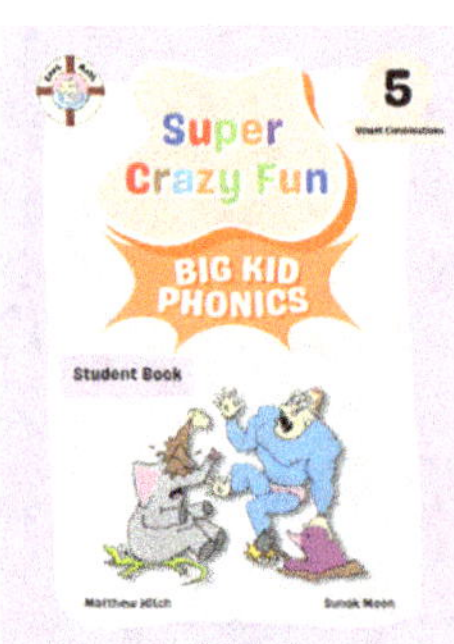

OUR SIGHT WORD FLASH CARDS!

don't

play

take

us

first

brush

bake

with

OUR SIGHT WORD FLASH CARDS!

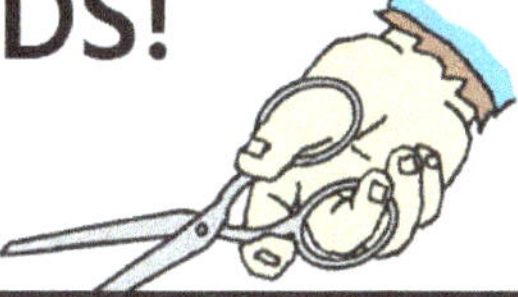

this	we
whose	make
new	be
best	can

OUR SIGHT WORD FLASH CARDS! 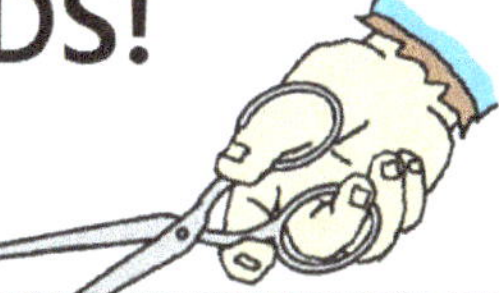

leave

at

but

after

even

next

hello

for

OUR SIGHT WORD FLASH CARDS! 

home	room
only	also
can't	is
ate	still

soup

lit

people

yell

his

poem

into

birthday

OUR SIGHT WORD FLASH CARDS! 

walk	maid
never	now
that	what
he	wear

OUR SIGHT WORD FLASH CARDS!

OUR SIGHT WORD FLASH CARDS!

not

the

one

to

your

like

go

has

Incidentally, the contents of all these phonics books are available in one big silly book, too:

Have a look in Amazon or check our website: www.supercrazyfun.net (or just search online in case our publishing options have increased since this was printed.)

www.ingramcontent.com/pod-product-compliance
Lightning Source LLC
Chambersburg PA
CBHW060123120726
48003CB00009B/2760